SWAMI B. V. TRIPURARI

Other books by Swāmī B. V. Tripurāri:

Aesthetic Vedanta
Ancient Wisdom for Modern Ignorance
Bhagavad-Gītā: Its Feeling and Philosophy
Form of Beauty
Gopāla-tāpanī Upaniṣad
Rasa: Love Relationships in Transcendence
Śrī Guru-Paramparā
Tattva-sandarbha
Śikṣāṣṭakam of Śrī Caitanya

For more information about the author, please contact:

Audarya
22001 Panorama Way
Philo, CA 95466

audarya@swami.org
www.harmonist.us
www.swamitripurari.com
www.swami.org

ISBN: 978-0-9849318-0-4

Printed in the U.S.A.

DEDICATION

To my spiritual master and dearmost friend,

Pūjyāpāda A. C. Bhaktivedānta Swāmī Prabhupāda.

TABLE OF CONTENTS

INTRODUCTION

*We cannot say that we do not exist. We cannot ex-
perience nonexistence. Although there are those who
would argue for the joy of no self, this book was
written primarily for those who sense that our individual existence is not something to do away with
in the name of enlightenment. Joy of Self is about our
identity in transcendence.[1]*

Recently a young man asked me about the ego. "If
the ego is so bad," he queried, "why do we have it in
the first place?" I told him that the ego is not bad, for
ego indicates identity. We all have an identity. We are
all individuals. However, our present sense of individuality is based on our identification with matter in the

1. For a discussion on consciousness as the authentic spiritual
self in relation to present-day materialistic theories in science
and philosophy that consider consciousness a material phe-
nomenon, please see my forthcoming publication Śrī Maṅgala
Sūtra Manas.

form of our bodies, minds, and the extensions of these in all that we call "ours." This identity is a false one, a false ego.

All of the major traditions of Eastern spirituality and many traditions of the West tell us in so many words that our present individual identity is based on material misidentification and is thereby false. What they do not tell us is what this book is about. They do not tell us that we have an individual identity to realize in transcendence once we have dissolved the false ego.

If material nature's offer for lasting joy is but false advertising, seeing through this sham is to see deeply. By moving from negative numbers to zero, we will feel that we have progressed. The Buddhist notion of fullness in emptiness stops at zero. There is no doubt a fullness in realizing the emptiness of material life, but can we progress from zero to positive numbers? If so, we will have to look even more deeply into the mystery of our self. So doing, devotional Vedānta informs us that we can realize the joy of self, the pure self, free from the exploitation that is characteristic of the false self born of material identification.

This book is an introduction to the devotional Vedānta of Śrī Chaitanya, Gauḍīya Vedānta. Śrī Chaitanya, the fifteenth-century Kṛṣṇa avatāra who personified a life of divine love, left in writing only eight Sanskrit stanzas. Yet his immediate followers churned these drops of nectar into an ocean of literature on divine love.

This introduction draws from their writings and the sacred literature of spiritual India such that anyone can gain a well-rounded acquaintance with the foundational philosophical principles of Gauḍīya Vedānta and thus come to know the potential for joy inherent in the self.

1. IN SEARCH OF JOY

Gaudīya Vedānta is a metanarrative that is deeply philosophical yet readily accessible to even the most common person. It speaks to us of joy and a life of love that never ends. If we embrace it, we will experience this love and never lose it due to the influence of time.

All living beings are in search of joy. We pursue joy directly and do so indirectly when we try to avoid distress. Although one of the four noble truths of the Buddha is that life is about suffering, the Buddha himself teaches how to end suffering, which is indirectly the pursuit of joy. So also are the masochists, sadists, and those labeled suicidal in search of joy. In this search for joy we are all one; we differ, however, in what our conception of joy is.

In another sense, we do all want the same type of joy: that which is everlasting. Therefore, it might be more accurate to say that we are looking for the same thing but looking in different places. Yet the joy we find in this world is fleeting at best.

Joy derived from material objects will never be everlasting. Why is this so? Material objects are transitory. Like foam on waves, material manifestations, from our small bodies to gigantic solar systems, appear for some time and disappear forever. Where do they go? From whence they came. We, on the other hand, are not the fleeting experience of material joy. We are the experiencers. We are consciousness and we possess consciousness, or the power of experiencing.

We often hear that absence of experience of the soul is justification for its dismissal. For the Vedāntin, however, experience itself is the soul. Experience is the function of consciousness, and consciousness is that which cannot be dismissed, since dismissal itself is a conscious act. We can dismiss all, from our own bodies to the entire universe, in our search for enduring joy, for all material manifestations will vanish. If, therefore, we are to be successful in our search for joy, we must look not to matter, but to the very consciousness of which we are constituted. To experience joy, we must find ourselves in the maze of matter.

The search for joy is in reality the search for self. It is only because we project our own self into material objects that we seem to derive pleasure from them. When we conceive of material objects as "mine," we in effect "enter" those objects and seem to derive pleasure from them. In reality, however, it is our self that has entered those objects, and it is the same self that is the basis of the joy we experience in relation to those objects. Thus close scrutiny reveals that it is consciousness alone in which pleasure is found, and we are a unit of consciousness. Yet how can we find ourselves and from whence do we come? These are the important questions for human society.

As human beings, we have the capacity to reason. In one sense the universal human language is that of reasoning. Unfortunately, all in human dress do not speak it. If we learn the language of reasoning and are thus directed by intelligence, we will reach the conclusion that logic itself is limited. It can lead us to the self, yet it cannot reveal the self, for intelligence is but a subtle material manifestation and is thus inferior to consciousness. Consciousness, the self, animates body, mind, and intelligence. It brings these gross and subtle material manifestations to life by lending itself to them. How then can intelligence be the guide of the soul? Our guide must possess greater knowledge than us. Thus intelligence cannot reveal the soul any more than a candle can shed light upon the sun. Intelligence can, however, point us in the self's direction, just as in darkness a candle can lead us to light.

As a ray of sun is separated from the sun by a cloud, we are apparently separated from our source by the cloud of illusion. The supreme sun—eternal joy and consciousness personified—is the source of both its own rays and the cloud of illusion. Thus, as rays of consciousness now illusioned by the cloud of ignorance, we must connect ourselves with our source and thus overcome the material illusion. In our search for joy we must find the reservoir of consciousness, with whom we are one yet at the same time different. To comprehend our inconceivable nature, we require help from beyond the limits of logic. We require more than human effort. We require grace, divine grace.

Although it may not be popular to advocate our dependence on another, when we understand this principle philosophically through the metanarrative of Gauḍīya Vedānta, we will realize the extent to which true independence is realized in divine dependence. Unlike Buddhism, monistic Vedānta, and other popular Eastern paths to perfection, Gauḍīya Vedānta is a devotional path with emphasis on grace. Gauḍīya Vedānta as exemplified by Śrī Chaitanya offers much to those who are in search of joy. He and his subsequent followers have presented a doctrine of divine love well reasoned and easily accessible to all. In our search for joy we would do well to consider its principal tenets.

2. AFFECTIONATE GUARDIAN

Godhead alone can guide us in our search, yet he chooses to do so through a particular agent. God is our guru, and yet our guru is not God. Although this may sound contradictory at first, Gauḍīya Vedānta makes clear this apparent contradiction, revealing a most charming notion of eternal guidance that can dispel all human apprehension.

In the modern world, we have seen a good number of totalitarian regimes and less-than-spiritual religious leaders. From politicians to popes, gestapos to gurus, we have learned to be cautious about claims of absolute knowledge. It is no wonder then that we are hesitant when Gauḍīya Vedānta speaks of the necessity of and utter dependence on the guru.

Who will mediate between humanity and divinity? Don't all souls have the potential for a personal relationship with God, without the need of a chaperone? In the language of love, "Three is a crowd." Furthermore, dependence on another, it would seem, hinders one from standing on one's own two feet. Can we not think for ourselves? Do the enlightened themselves have gurus? If they had any necessity at some point in their eternal progress, it would seem at best that such necessity was a relative one, rendering the principle of guru dispensable at some point. All of these doubts and misconceptions regarding the principle of guru must be cleared up if we are to be successful in our search, for the guru is an eternal necessity for all souls.

Gurus are, in the simplest of terms, teachers. What do they teach? They teach how to serve God. To do so, they themselves must be servants of the Godhead. If they teach service to God, what have we to fear from them? If, on the other hand, they teach service to themselves and take the position of being the enjoyers of all of our service, there is good cause for reservation. If they teach that they are God, they are not gurus.

Those who posit absolute monism teach that all individuality is illusion. For such monists, all is ultimately "one" and there is no other. In place of this doctrine of absolute monism, *Joy of Self* suggests a more nuanced understanding of ultimate reality that finds room for individuality without compromising unity. The text posits a form of devotional Vedanta—a doctrine of wise love—in which the individual self unites in love with its source, experiencing a unity of will with the Absolute: a oneness in purpose but a nuanced ontological difference in identity.

The philosophy of monism posits that atomic particles of consciousness are but an appearance, an illusion. This philosophy has been thoroughly dealt with in the many writings of Gauḍīya Vedānta's self-realized *ācāryas*, or spiritual masters. It would be prudent for the serious spiritual aspirant to go through both these *ācāryas'* commentaries on sacred literature, such as *Bhagavad-gītā* and *Śrīmad Bhāgavatam*, as well as the books they themselves have authored. It should suffice herein to underscore the tenet of the Gauḍīya Vaiṣṇavas that the atomic soul is not an illusion, while at the same time in material life the soul is absorbed in an illusory identity. Removing this illusory identity in the context of the culture of devotional Vedanta, we realize our likeness to the Godhead but not that we ourselves are the entirety of the Absolute. In the latter conception, both God and atomic soul ultimately cease to have any relevance, as does any means of such realization. In later chapters these important points will be dealt with in greater detail.

Although gurus are not God, neither are they to be considered as merely atomic souls bound in the net of material illusion. Gurus are servants of God as are all souls, yet they are servants who have realized the truth of their eternal servanthood. With regard to service, it should be noted that service in itself is not a bad thing. The value of service depends on who is served. If it is indeed God whom we are taught to serve, such service is in no way demeaning, for the Godhead is the perfect object of love. Service reposed in God through the agency of guru is the most dignified engagement for all souls. Those who conceive of themselves as nothing more than eternal servants of the Godhead represented in their own guru are fit to serve in the capacity of guru themselves.

Gurus are those souls who have emptied themselves of all selfish considerations arising from material misidentification. As such, they are filled with the spiritual *śakti*, energy of Godhead, to do God's work in this world. As the ambassador of the United States is highly regarded in a foreign country, similarly the guru, although not God himself, should nonetheless be highly honored, for it is God alone whom the guru represents. Moreover, gurus represent Godhead in the manner in which God chooses to interact with humanity. Thus in one sense gurus are more important to us than God himself, yet they never think themselves so.

Real gurus have no disciples, though many see themselves as such, and gurus honor their vision, inspired as it is by the Godhead. Their own angle of vision is that they are servants of all, for all are but parts and parcels of God. They do not see others independently of their relationship with the Absolute. Their task is thus to share this vision with all whom they encounter.

Gurus are our bright spiritual prospect appearing before us to instruct us through both precept and practice. Their affection for the bound souls is itself without bounds. They never tire of revealing the spiritual reality. Thus genuine spiritual aspirants are forced not by ordinary law but by all reason and ultimately love and affection to submit to the guru's instruction and to love *śrī guru* eternally, for who could have shown us greater love?

How shall we find such an affectionate guardian? Because the path of devotion and transcendence has been traversed by others, a map has been charted and left for us to follow. On that map, first and foremost we are directed to the information counter. Sacred literature charts our course, and in doing so, points us in the direction of *śrī guru*, the captain of our ship. From sacred literature we can learn the qualifications of the agent of the Absolute, and therein we are implored to take the guru's shelter. With these two, map and guide, scripture and guru, on the boat of our human birth, fueled by the wind of our own sincerity, we are well equipped to cross the ocean of material suffering and reach the shore of eternal joy.

3. REVEALED SOUND

The concept of scripture is no less difficult for modern society to embrace than that of śrī guru. Yet scripture is as inseparable from the eternal guide as the sun is inseparable from our eyes in our attempt to see. If the guru and saint are our eyes, scripture is the sun. If all three are in place, we can see.

From the scripture we learn the qualifications of the guru, whose every word must be backed by scriptural reference for it to have spiritual standing. This is so because the scripture is the eternal reality manifest in sound to the seers and written down by them to uplift us. As such, scripture is eternal. It manifests and at times is unmanifest, as is the world itself.

The many now interested in what has been called "Eastern mysticism" are wrong in construing that such teachings are mystical rather than rational and based on

11

the scripture. Christianity has been long and accurately
portrayed as a rational, scripturally based doctrine, but
no less so is the theism of the Orient. Outside of atheistic
doctrines such as Buddhism and Jainism, practically all
branches of Indian philosophy draw heavily from sacred
literature, the Vedas and Purāṇas.

Although there is a similarity between the sacred
literature of the Orient and the Christian Bible, the Jew-
ish Torah, and the Islamic Koran, there is considerable
difference as well. The difference lies primarily in the
Oriental notion of the eternality of the Veda. While the
Bible, Torah, and Koran all have a beginning in time, the
Veda is held to be beginningless. The fact that it is written
down by human hand does not compromise its eternality.

The Veda is Brahman, the Absolute, in sound. It is
the Absolute extending itself to humanity, perfection
speaking to the imperfect. By imperfect means, we who
are steeped in imperfection stand little chance of know-
ing that which is perfect. Both our sense perception by
which we "know" and the logic that extends our knowledge beyond that which we can perceive with the senses
are imperfect instruments.

Sense perception is as flawed as are the senses themselves. With our eyes alone we will never know the size
and nearness of the full moon at night. Yet with the help
of reasoning we can understand that it is large, its apparent smallness owing to its being situated at a great dis-
tance. Yet as sense perception is faulty, so is reasoning

lacking. This is so because unless we can validate that our reasoning is true in all circumstances, that it has universal concomitance, we cannot say that it is absolutely true. Demonstrating this universal concomitance is virtually impossible for practically any logical inference.

How then can we know for certain? How can we arrive at perfect knowledge and thus be perfectly happy? Only if perfect knowledge cares to reveal itself to we who are imperfect. The finite soul can never know the infinite save and except if the infinite, out of its infinite capacity, chooses to reveal itself to the finite. Perfect knowledge is just that, perfect, and therefore it is worshippable by those steeped in imperfection. We will never be successful in attempts to arrest perfect knowledge and imprison it within the jail cell of our human embodiment, for its own agenda is to liberate us from our finite conception. It makes this agenda known to us through the Veda, which is etymologically derived from the Sanskrit root *vid,* which means to know as well as to make known. The Veda is thus that which makes itself known and by which all can know conclusively.

The Veda does not claim that by studying its words with our intellect we will know the truth. It does not attempt to establish that which is eternally self-established. It is the self-established truth imploring us to take up the means of experiencing the truth ourselves. By this alone shall we know, yet hearing from those who have themselves seen is tantamount to seeing oneself.

The Veda, eternal sound, is experienced by the seers beyond the confines of time and space. Returning to time and space, they share their vision with us, thus serving as first-hand witnesses to the truth. Without them and without the Veda, we will never know the truth, for from those who have seen we derive the necessary inspiration to see for ourselves. They also give us a proper conceptual orientation, the systematic means of pursuit, and information regarding the goal. These three, known as *sambhanda*, *abidheya*, and *prayojana*, are the essential elements of sacred literature, and a brief explanation of these elements comprises the balance of this short book.

4. CONCEPTUAL ORIENTATION

The term sambandha literally means "relationship." In the context of Gauḍīya Vedānta, it represents knowledge of the relationship between the world and God, God and the atomic souls, the atomic souls and the world, and so on. In the Śrīmad-Bhāgavatam, the essence of the Veda, all knowledge that concerns the nature of the Absolute and his energies as well as the activities of those energies is considered sambandha-jñāna.

Although the Absolute as described in the *Bhāgavata* is one without a second, he is not without energy. The existence of the Absolute is a dynamic affair on account of his being possessed of various energies. Just as we are all possessed of energy by which we conduct our affairs, so the Absolute is replete with energies. The oneness of the Absolute, however, is not compromised by its possessing energy, for although we can speak of energetic and energy as different, they are at the same time inseparable.

In the monistic schools of Vedānta, the Absolute is portrayed as devoid of energy. Monists conceive of the Godhead as such because they cannot understand how an Absolute replete with energy can at the same time be singular. The unfortunate result of pursuing this line of reasoning is, among other things, that all that we see and experience, including the sense of our own individuality, is rendered an illusion. Moreover, the material experience is considered an illusion that has no logical explanation. The material experience is false knowledge purported to have no knower and no known.

Gauḍīya Vedānta can save us from this confusion. Explaining the Absolute as presented in the *Bhāgavata*, Gauḍīya Vedānta posits an Absolute that is singular in principle yet plural in terms of experience. The Godhead's experience of himself is made possible by his inherent energies. Because these energies have no independent existence from the Godhead, they are in this sense one with him. The happy result of this conception is that a logical explanation of the world of our present experience follows. The material world is understood to be the external energy of the Godhead. Furthermore, our own sense of individuality is validated, we being an atomic particle of the Godhead's marginal energy.

In touch with the external energy, the marginal energy brings about the world as we know it. While matter is insentient, sentient beings bring matter to life. The atomic souls animate the material world, which like a movie has a beginning and an end. Although the movie ends, karmic reruns play endlessly with the same actors in new roles. As atomic souls reincarnate life after life due to their misidentification with matter, they are unaware of their predicament due to the deluding influence of the external power of Godhead. Material nature rules over the atomic souls, even though her capacity to do so is initially dependent on her being animated by them. The relationship between the marginal and external powers of Godhead can be compared to a person in the modern world turning on the insentient television only to have it then take over his life.

In this life of material despair, we may misconstrue that we are happy. Yet time tells us that the happier we are, based on material security, possessions, friends, and family, the more miserable we will be when they all slip through our fingers, and our own attachment to temporary things forces us to remain in a temporal plane in search of eternity. Birth and death are not friends of those in quest of the fountain of youth. Yet it is these two whom we must contend with as long as we insist upon the kingdom of God without God.

In conjunction with the external energy, the activities of the atomic souls, parts and parcels of the Godhead's marginal energy, are illusory, however profoundly we may speak of them. Although units of eternity and joy, conscious atomic souls such as ourselves are trapped in a network of illusion. Identifying with the external energy of Godhead, we repeatedly experience the tribulations of birth and death. The solution to our plight lies first in knowledge, not only of this predicament, but even more so in knowledge of the Godhead himself.

The Godhead has his own primary energy by which he conducts his affairs aloof from the material atmosphere. These affairs are termed *līlā* in the *Bhāgavata*. They are untouched by the external energy and are thus never subject to the misery that we experience due to the external energy. Because we are constituted of the marginal energy, we can live either under the influence of the external energy of Godhead or under the influence of his primary energy. The former is the life of misery we are now experiencing, the latter the life of joy we are in search of.

Who is this Godhead possessed of primary, external, and marginal powers? The *Bhāgavata* tells us that it is Kṛṣṇa. Kṛṣṇa means "all attractive," "irresistible." Kṛṣṇa is joy himself. Because he is so, he also is known in terms of his cognitive and existential features, as Brahman and Paramātmā respectively.

For one to exist, one need not be cognizant. If, however, one is cognizant, one must exist as well. One can exist and be cognizant without being joyful. But if one is joyful in nature, one must exist and be cognizant as well. Because Kṛṣṇa is nothing short of joy itself, out of necessity this singular, absolute person is also known in two other features. As cognizance he is known as Brahman, and as existence, Paramātmā. In his Paramātmā feature, he manifests and presides over the material world and enters the heart of every atomic soul as a witness to all. In his Brahman feature, he brings material existence to life.

These two features of Kṛṣṇa are realized by those who tread the paths of yoga and knowledge *(jñāna)* respectively. Those who tread the path of devotion know him as Bhagavān, or he who possesses all attractiveness. These devoted transcendentalists know this ultimate feature of the Absolute in two ways, either through devotion steeped in awe and reverence *(vaidhī-bhakti)* as the majestic Godhead appearing in innumerable incarnations or through passionate love *(rāgānugā-bhakti)* as Kṛṣṇa, the charming humanlike lover.

Kṛṣṇa, the charming humanlike Godhead, is the ultimate object of love, depicted by the Gauḍīya Vedāntins as an eternal youth, the rural cowherder of dark complexion resembling a rain cloud. As the cloud is pregnant with rain, Kṛṣṇa is full in himself yet showering love in all directions and celebrating his fullness, and in this way nourishing all. Kṛṣṇa is the God of the Vedānta of aesthetics, not a dry philosophical principle but the ultimate person—infinitely beautiful, charming, soft-hearted, yet strong willed. He has innumerable transcendental qualities and engages in pastimes with his eternal retinue. Flute-bearing, he charms his devotees with passionate spiritual love free from material contamination. He is the perfect object of love because all potential for love in transcendence can be realized in him. When Kṛṣṇa becomes the object of one's love, one can realize not only love steeped in a reverence that is appropriate for the greatest of persons, but love in friendship, the filial love one feels for one's child, and, in the optimum, passionate love for God. Kṛṣṇa is thus the supreme Godhead, the acme of theism and transcendental realization, in that it is love that we all seek in eternity. Being the perfect object of love, Kṛṣṇa is thus objectively supreme through an analysis of love.

Kṛṣṇa is surrounded by his primary energy appearing as his own family, friends, abode, and paraphernalia. This primary energy ultimately personifies the potency of pleasure, *hlādinī*. Known also as Rādhā, Kṛṣṇa's eternal consort, she is the shelter of ultimate love. The object of love, Śrī Kṛṣṇa, and the shelter of love, Śrī Rādhā, together constitute the Godhead as complimentary features of the Absolute. There is no meaning to Kṛṣṇa without Rādhā and no meaning to Rādhā without Kṛṣṇa. In the eternal drama of their transcendental lives, we can play a small yet infinitely important part.

The conceptual orientation presented in the *Bhāgavata* offers great hope to suffering humanity. It tells us that we can experience eternal love in relation to Kṛṣṇa, the object of perfect love. Love for Kṛṣṇa stands as a perfect example of the highest love. The reality of Rādhā-Kṛṣṇa speaks sweetly, assuring us of all that we aspire for, should we but turn in the right direction. To live in perfect love and joy is possible when we repose our loving propensity in Rādhā-Kṛṣṇa. All other attempts for love are futile, for they are off-center at best. Time tells us that nothing belongs to us. Gauḍīya Vedānta tells us that everything belongs to Kṛṣṇa. Loving Kṛṣṇa enables us to transcend the false proprietorship that has imprisoned us within time and space, leaving self-centered material consciousness forever and entering the land of love.

5. THE MEANS

In accordance with our conceptual orientation, sambandha, we will act. This action is the means, abhidheya, by which we can achieve our goal. All that the Bhāgavata deals with in terms of achieving its stated goal, as well as that activity which inhibits us from doing so, falls under the category of abhidheya. The goal is love of Kṛṣṇa, which constitutes the highest joy, and the means is devotion to Kṛṣṇa. Acts adverse to devotion are those to be avoided.

The *Bhāgavata* defines the best means as that which completely satisfies the Supreme Self. If God is pleased, so will we, his parts and parcels, be satisfied. Devotion to Kṛṣṇa that is free from ulterior motive and uninterrupted is that which satisfies Kṛṣṇa. Devotion in which something other than the pleasure of the Supreme is desired is called mixed devotion *(miśrā bhakti)*. Devotion

23

can be mixed with worldly desires *(karma-miśrā bhakti)*, the desire for liberation *(jñāna-miśrā bhakti)*, or the desire for mystic perfection *(yoga-miśrā bhakti)*. All of these types of *bhakti* are not pure, or unmotivated. They bring results to their respective practitioners in the form of good *karma*, liberation, and mystic perfection. They do not, however, afford their practitioners love of Godhead.

The path of *karma* focuses on material betterment, the path of knowledge upon liberation. The path of yoga is concerned with liberation, as well as acquiring mystic power. The path of pure devotion, however, is not about acquiring anything other than devotion itself. It is thus to be executed for its own improvement. It is a spiritual and thus eternal means to a spiritual end.

The *Bhāgavata* speaks of the socio-religious system of *varṇāśrama-dharma*. This is the religious way of life also known as the path of *karma*, whereby we can prosper in this life and the next. It organizes society in consideration of *karmic* propensities, both in terms of occupation as well as spiritual pursuit. This conception of *dharma* is only successfully executed if as a result of one's observance of its tenets one enters the path of pure devotion *(śuddha-bhakti)*.

Although participation in the socio-religious system requires many prerequisites, this is not the case on the path of pure devotion. Similarly, other paths aimed at transcendence of birth and death, such as the paths of yoga and knowledge, also require that participants meet various prerequisites. To practice yoga properly, one must observe celibacy. The path of knowledge requires purity of heart, renunciation, and equal vision. These are not easy things to achieve. Pure devotion, however, can be cultivated from the time one has awakened faith in Kṛṣṇa.

It is noteworthy that efficacy in any of these paths requires a mixture of devotion. Without devotion, the practitioners in these systems will not achieve their desired goals. It is devotion, therefore, that is the means in all respects.

The paths of *karma*, yoga, and knowledge are not helpful to pure devotion. Before pure devotion has awakened in the heart, practice borrowed from these paths may be helpful in the same way that pushing a car whose battery has died will help to start the car. Once the car is started, however, of what use will pushing be? Similarly, once pure devotion has awakened in the heart, it cannot be helped by anything else. Moreover, only when devotion is free from the tendencies born of *karma*, knowledge, and yoga can it be said to be pure.

Devotional service to Kṛṣṇa can be practiced in all circumstances, at all times, and by all living entities. This further attests to its spiritual nature. The *Bhāgavatam* is ripe with examples of persons engaging in devotional service to Kṛṣṇa in even the most adverse circumstances. Prahlāda Mahārāja, for example, performed *bhakti* in his mother's womb.

With regard to time, the *Bhāgavatam* also gives examples of persons engaging in devotional service from the beginning to the end of time, from creation to annihilation. Devotional service is even engaged in after liberation by those who have perfected their devotional culture. Devotional service, although primarily the prerogative of human society, also overflows into animal and plant society. When devotees engage in devotional service, animals such as cows, whose milk is offered to the deity of Kṛṣṇa, also participate in *bhakti*, as do plants when offered to the deity. Such animals and plants, however, cannot practice yoga or culture knowledge of the Absolute. One cannot perform yoga at all times, such as during sleep, nor does the practice of yoga continue after liberation. Similarly, the culture of knowledge insists on many prerequisites and cannot be performed in all circumstances.

Devotional service to Kṛṣṇa has three divisions: devotional service in practice *(sadhana-bhakti)*, devotional service in ecstasy *(bhāva-bhakti)*, and devotional service in love of God *(prema-bhakti)*. Devotion to Kṛṣṇa is also divided into devotion guided by scriptural injunction *(vaidhī-bhakti)* and spontaneous devotion *(rāgānugā-bhakti)*.

Śrī Chaitanya has emphasized spontaneous devotion. His disciples, the legendary six *goswāmīs* of Vṛndāvana, have demonstrated in their writings based on the *Bhāgavata* how spiritual aspirants can cultivate spontaneous devotion. Generally one is required to embrace regulative devotional service with a view to gradually develop spontaneous devotion. In the material world the soul is spontaneously moving in the direction of material pursuit. This spontaneity can be harnessed by regulative devotion and through spiritual practices directed to Kṛṣṇa. Gradually one's devotion for Kṛṣṇa will be as spontaneous as a young girl's love for a young boy.

In devotional service in practice, one follows the guidelines of the guru and gradually cleanses one's heart of material desire. When the heart is almost free of *karmic* influences, one becomes fixed in devotion. One then develops a taste for devotional practices and gradually begins to hanker for a particular loving relationship with Kṛṣṇa. One may like to serve Kṛṣṇa as a servant, friend, well-wisher, or lover. At this stage one passes from devotional service in practice to devotional service in ecstasy and experiences deep spiritual emotions that, when cultivated, bring one to the perfection of devotional service in love of God.

The principal practice of devotional service is chanting the names of God. This chanting is performed in group singing *(kīrtana)* with musical accompaniment. Śrī Chaitanya accompanied his group chanting with hand cymbals and a simple clay drum indigenous to West Bengal. These instruments are considered eternal participants in group chanting. Other instruments may also be used, yet one must be careful to distinguish between a musical presentation and that which is spiritual. Too much emphasis on the musical and instrumental accompaniment may shift the focus of the chanting from the *mantra* to the instruments and melody, thus rendering it less than spiritual. To avoid this problem, the chanting should be performed under the auspices of a pure devotee of Kṛṣṇa.

The pure devotee is the guru who initiates the disciple. At that time the disciple is given a rosary of 108 beads and is instructed to chant the Kṛṣṇa *mantra* on the rosary a prescribed number of times daily. The disciple is also engaged in ritualistic devotion in the temple of Kṛṣṇa. In this way the disciple engages throughout the day in hearing and chanting about Kṛṣṇa and carrying out the instruction of the guru. This may find a disciple engaged in a wide variety of services all for the pleasure of Kṛṣṇa. As the disciple's consciousness is purified, he or she learns to meditate internally upon Kṛṣṇa twenty-four hours a day.

Many persons interested in devotional service are not able to take up the life of devotion described above. They can, however, accept initiation from the guru. They can learn to chant Kṛṣṇa's name in their homes and sacrifice what time and energy they can for the mission of Śrī Chaitanya. The guru will give them guidelines to follow in their home life. As they consciously make sacrifices for Kṛṣṇa in the form of time and financial support

for his mission, their hearts become gradually purified
of the false notion of proprietorship. As they realize that
everything belongs to Kṛṣṇa, they too can take up the
life of devotion and eventually attain love of Kṛṣṇa.

6. THE GOAL

The fruit of devotional service is love of Kṛṣṇa. As such, all sections of the Bhāgavatam that deal directly with the experience of love of God, as well as those sections that deal with the fruits of religion (dharma), economic development (artha), sense enjoyment (kāma), and liberation (mokṣa), constitute direct and indirect descriptions of the goal (prayojana).

In describing the fruits of activities other than pure devotion, the *Bhāgavatam* seeks to point out indirectly the glory of love of Kṛṣṇa, for the fruits of religion, economic development, sense gratification, and even liberation from the cycle of birth and death are paltry in comparison.

Joy is our stated or unstated goal of life. The joy derived from love of Kṛṣṇa is the highest kind of joy. It is joy that is derived from making the perfect object of love one's loving repose. This joy is the opposite of material joy, in which one makes one's own joy the goal, misconstruing oneself to be the body and mind. In transcendental love, the satisfaction of Kṛṣṇa's transcendental senses is the only thought of the perfect devotees. They do not seek joy independent of the joy of the Absolute. While material joy is selfish and self-centered, the joy derived from love of Kṛṣṇa is based on sacrifice, giving, and the self-forgetfulness that true love calls for, and thus it constitutes the highest love.

The question arises, however, as to how it is that the Absolute is in need of anything. How does Śrī Kṛṣṇa derive pleasure from those who love him? Is he not full in himself to begin with? He is indeed, yet as we have seen, he is surrounded by his own inner energy *(svarūpa-śakti)*, with whom he eternally consorts. His inner power manifests as eternal associates in five primary moods with whom he eternally enjoys the bliss of his own nature. The five primary moods are known as *bhakti-rasa*, aesthetic rapture in transcendence.

The *Bhāgavatam* describes the Absolute philosophically as well as through aesthetic analysis. According to the Indian discipline of aesthetics, the soul of aesthetic experience is termed *rasa*. In the Upaniṣads the Absolute is also described by this term, *raso vai saḥ*, "The Absolute is aesthetic experience." The *Bhāgavatam* develops this concept. It is thus both a book of Vedānta philosophy and one concerned with aesthetics. It is a philosophy of

beauty, the truth that is beauty. It directs us to Kṛṣṇa and
the possibility of entering a transcendental relationship
with the Absolute, the possibility of experiencing *rasa*.

Bhakti rasa develops in the atomic soul in the course
of cultivating one of five primary emotions directed to
the perfect object of love, Kṛṣṇa. These primary Kṛṣṇa-
centered emotions are the essence of Kṛṣṇa's eternal
associates *(pārṣadas),* who are constituted of his inner
power. Thus atomic souls can enter into the eternal love
affair of the Absolute by taking shelter of Śrī Kṛṣṇa's inner power, manifest as his eternal associates.

The five primary *rasas* are neutrality *(śānta),* servitor-
ship *(dāsya),* friendship *(sakhya),* parental love *(vātsalya),*
and conjugal love *(mādhurya).* Thus one can love Kṛṣṇa
in neutrality, as a servant, as a friend, as his well-wisher,
and as his lover. Śrī Chaitanya has revealed that conjugal love for Kṛṣṇa is the best amongst transcendental
achievements.

Kṛṣṇa's consorts thus exemplify to the fullest
extent the life of transcendental love. All of the other
transcendental *rasas* in effect serve as a necessary
background for the eternal drama of conjugal love
of Godhead enacted between Rādhā and Kṛṣṇa. This
drama takes place in the guise of humanity, as Śrī
Kṛṣṇa, the Supreme Truth, comes so close to his part
and parcels that the affair at a glance seems no more
than the love of a young village boy and girl. However,
it is much more than this and is certainly free from

all material inebriety. The land, water, trees, animals, birds, and people in this transcendental drama *(līlā)* are all supra-mundane. Nothing there is touched by material illusion, and one can realize this dimension of consciousness and experience the highest joy only when one is free from the selfishness that makes for a material life of unhappiness. While selfishness is the basis of the material plane of consciousness, selflessness forms the basis of the spiritual dimension of consciousness—Kṛṣṇa consciousness. This is our highest prospect, within which lies the joy of self.